HAYNES EXPLAINS
FESTIVALS
Owners' Workshop Manual

© Haynes Publishing • Written by **Boris Starling**

Published in April 2020

A catalogue record for this book is available from the British Library

ISBN 978 1 78521 692 3

Haynes Publishing, Sparkford, Yeovil,
Somerset BA22 7JJ, UK
Tel: +44 (0) 1963 440635
Website: www.haynes.com

Haynes North America, Inc.,
861 Lawrence Drive, Newbury Park,
California 91320, USA

Printed and bound in Malaysia

Cover image from Getty Images

Illustrations taken
from the Haynes MGA
Owners Workshop Manual

Written by **Boris Starling**
Edited by **Louise McIntyre**
Designed by **Richard Parsons**

Safety first!

From a health and safety point of view, festivals are a nightmare. Improperly secured tent guy ropes can cause falls which lead to minor injuries and the necessity of first aid. Alcohol and narcotics may cause those who consume them to become briefly, or not-so-briefly, mindless. The standard of sanitation in toilet blocks varies between sub-optimal and Chernobyl. Worst of all, you can't even stand out in your hi-viz gear as 10,000 people thinking they're back in San Francisco c. 1968 will be wearing tie-dye T-shirts in exactly the same shades of orange and yellow.

Working facilities

For the performers: a large stage with raised dais for the drummer, plenty of space for the lead guitarist to prowl around during his solos, a much smaller space for the bassist to stand still and look moody, and a runway for the singer to perform a risky and rather graceless stage dive. For the crowds: a space roughly half the size of minimum personal space requirements, and never more than 5' away from someone with BO, halitosis, or both. In tents: space-sharing with rucksacks, crates of cider and WHO THE HELL IS THAT AND WHERE DID THEY COME FROM?

Contents

Introduction

There are certain markers of the British summer which are as constant as the North Star. First, that there will be a brief heatwave (inevitably accompanied by tabloid 'Phew What A Scorcher!' headlines above stories about how Britain is hotter than Ibiza/Brazil/Hell) and everyone will lose their minds and act as though it's never happened before. Second, an English sporting team will somehow contrive to snatch defeat from the jaws of victory in a preposterously unlikely fashion. And third, there will be music festivals.

The UK festival industry is now worth more than £2bn, and there are more than 200 music festivals every summer. Glastonbury is the most famous, of course – for a few days Worthy Farm has a population roughly the size of Ipswich – but it is very much *primus inter pares* rather than an unchallenged outlier. (A bit of Latin for you all there – 'first among equals' – and not to be confused with any of the following: a Primus stove, which is a staple of festival camping; a football team from Milan; or a misspelled capital of France.)

The sheer number of festivals makes the market extremely competitive. A festival organiser can no longer get away with hiring a skiffle band from the local pub, paying them in cider and hoping that a jury-rigged sound system lasts the weekend without blowing up and/or setting light to every field within a five-mile radius. There's a constant pressure to sign good bands and/or come up with innovations to keep the festival feeling fresh and relevant.

All this is, of course, good news for the festival goer – up to a point, at any rate. The laws of supply and demand mean that there wouldn't be this many festivals if there weren't enough people who wanted to go to them, which in turn means that the popular ones are hideously oversubscribed. Glastonbury tickets seem to sell out in about five seconds flat, meaning that you're almost certainly going to miss out unless you get extremely lucky with the website.

No matter which festival you choose, there's a thin line between having the time of your life and the worst time of your life. Haynes Explains is here to help you walk that line, Johnny Cash-style, and ensure that when you return to the real world after your festival experience you can tell people with a straight face that it was much more peace and love than mud and misery.

Dimensions, weights and capacities

Overall length

Of a festival in total.. between 1 and 4 days, depending

Of the time spent sober in that festival .... 17% of total time

Of the queue for the toilet block on Saturday evening 1.14 miles

Overall height

Of a pissed woman balancing unsteadily on her
equally pissed boyfriend's shoulders, aggregate ...... 9' 8"

Of a summer's worth of festival wristbands
piled on top of each other .... 26.9 cm

Of Liam Gallagher's microphone stand .... always 3" taller than him

Consumption

Cider or beer.... 1 can per hour for at least 12 hours. You have to pace yourself
here, you know. Slow and steady does it. There are no prizes
for being the muppet who sets off at a rate of knots and then
keels over two hours before The Killers come on stage.

Drugs .... again, know your limits. You're not Keith Richards (or if you actually
are, hi Keith, nice to know you're reading Haynes Explains), and nor
are you Tony Montana in Scarface. Also, they're still illegal, and
though the police are reasonably tolerant when it comes to some
drugs (as long as it's personal use only), others will land you in trouble.

Engine

Stroke .... one-fifth of the band The Strokes. Julian Casablancas, Nick Valensi,
Albert Hammond Jr, Nikolai Fraiture – bass and Fabrizio Moretti all
represent one Stroke each.

Power................. 72 MLA speakers for main hangs, 8 MLA Compacts for stereo infill at
pit barrier, 4 x 14 MLA delay positions.

Torque .... Needed to twist the lid off a jar which has so far proved unopenable
and has led to huge arguments as to whether you really need gherkins
at a festival anyway.

Reasons to purchase

1) Creating memories

Festivals are gatherings, brief moments of communal togetherness in an increasingly atomised world. Twenty years from now you won't remember just another night in the pub, but you will remember four days at a festival (unless you had such a good time that you can't remember a thing). The stories will get taller with each retelling, and the bad memories will be gradually sidelined in favour of the good ones. This is the stuff of which friendships are made. This, and 16-hour marathons on FIFA '19, of course. As DJ Edith Bowman said: 'When I think of festivals I think of the people I was with first, then the music.'

2) The outfits

Fashion blogs, magazines, Pinterest boards: you name it, there's endless inspiration for festival outfits out there. Think of a festival as a giant fancy-dress party. You can wear things you wouldn't normally choose or dare to, safe in the knowledge that you almost certainly won't be the most outrageously dressed person within the nearest few square metres, let alone all of the festival. Basically it's like Torture Garden but with much less rubber and leather (way too hot for even an English summer, don't you know?) Oh – face paint and glitter. More of both than at any party you've ever been to since the age of six.

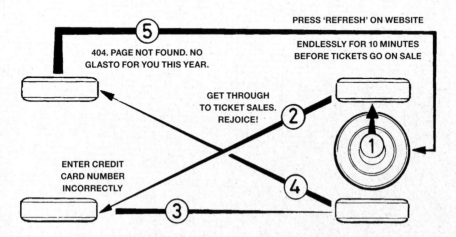

FIG 17•1 **BOOKING GLASTONBURY TICKETS**

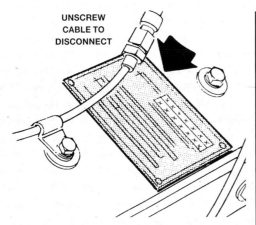

UNSCREW
CABLE TO
DISCONNECT

FIG 17·2 **TURN ON, TUNE IN, DROP OUT**

3) A sense of freedom

So much of life is routine, and festivals are a break from that. Put down your phone (overloaded mobile networks may force you into this whether you want to or not). Start drinking at breakfast time. Eat whatever you like. Talk to new people – most people are super-friendly at festivals, and some of them may even become lifelong friends (or perhaps ill-considered sexual partners for the weekend, or maybe both). Throw off your mental chains, as Howard Jones once said. If Howard himself is appearing at your festival, he'll probably sing that line to you in the flesh. As with the glitter and face paint, access your inner child, as that inner child certainly doesn't make an appearance in departmental meetings, working on corporate spreadsheets or the 1721 back to Orpington.

Discover new music

When you go to a concert – sorry, when you go to a gig (Haynes Explains revealing our advanced years and lack of cool there) – you get to see only the artist or group in question (and maybe their warm-up act too). At a festival there are scores of them. Most of them won't set your world on fire, but even if one or two do, that's one or two more than you'd otherwise have known. And perhaps one of these lesser-known acts might go on to be a global megastar, and you can say in all seriousness that you loved them before they were famous.

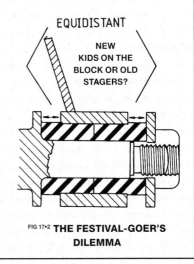

EQUIDISTANT

NEW
KIDS ON THE
BLOCK OR OLD
STAGERS?

FIG 17·2 **THE FESTIVAL-GOER'S DILEMMA**

Consider your purchase

The travel writer Ernest Thesiger, when asked about his memories of World War One, is reputed to have replied: 'My dear, the noise! And the people!' Much of both could also apply to music festivals. Here are several reasons not to go anywhere near them.

1) The mud

Heed the words of Liam Gallagher. 'I know everyone bangs on about the mud like, "it's great" and all that. No it ain't. There's nothing great about mud. If it's going to be muddy, I'm cancelling. Someone else can have that slot, I'm not having mud.'

N = (E – 183), WHERE E IS HOW MANY YOU NEED AND N HOW MANY YOU HAVE

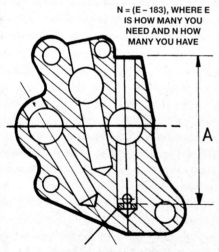

A

FIG 17•4 **PORTABLE TOILET DISTRIBUTION: A USER'S SCHEMATIC**

2) The toilets

More on this – much more on this - in Exhaust Systems, but suffice to say that the UN inspectors searching for biological weapons in Iraq before the Gulf War were looking in entirely the wrong place. A quick visit to the toilets at any music festival would have revealed the kind of germinating plagues that could make the world look like an apocalypse movie in about three days flat.

3) Hygiene

Put simply, there isn't any. Within two days you'll smell like the lovechild of a polecat and a skunk. Within three you will be trying to get upwind of yourself. Good news: everyone around you will smell just as bad. Bad news: this olfactory mutually assured destruction will last only for the duration of the festival. The moment you're back in the real world but haven't yet found a bath (for self) and an incinerator (for your clothes), you will be among people who have nodding acquaintance with the twin concepts of soap and deodorant, and who will afford you an exclusion zone roughly the size of the one around Fukushima. Small children will run screaming from your presence. Dogs will howl as though mourning the loss of an entire canine species.

4) Getting a posse together

Yeah, say about 193 of your friends, that sounds great, let's go to a festival. Then one by one they remember (or 'remember') that they can't make it that weekend, or they might be able to depending on their sister's boyfriend's second cousin's hairdresser's childminder's petsitter, and even the ones that say yes can't pay you for the tickets right now, and by the time you actually get to the festival (which is usually an ordeal in itself) you've had more than 2,000 WhatsApp messages from your mates and 27 calls from your bank (if your bank manager wasn't on the phone before you set out for the festival, he certainly will be by the time you get back). AND IS IT REALLY WORTH IT?

5) The camera never lies, but the software does

Celebrities at festivals manage to look great on Instagram because they have people – 'glam squads' – whose sole purpose in life is to make those celebrities look like that. Non-celebrities (i.e. you) don't have glam squads, and therefore your Instagram shots will be equally lacking in comparison. The only filters capable of hiding the filth, sunburn and exhaustion are either so strong that they make you look like a cartoon character or so dark that you're a silhouette from a 1920s vampire film.

Anti-capitalism?

Festivals like to pose as bucolic idylls of anti-capitalism, but in reality they could hardly be more corporate if they tried. They have sponsorship. They have higher-bracket taxpayers bellowing their love for Jeremy Corbyn even though they wouldn't vote for him in a month of Sundays. To quote the journalist Toby Young: 'By some sleight of hand, festivals have retained their countercultural cachet that dates back to the 1960s, even though they're about as "alternative" as a five-bedroom house in Kew. Which, come to think of it, is the sort of house most festival-goers live in when they're not in a bell tent or a tepee.'

Several hundred quid on the ticket, more for transport there, and that's before you even factor in the intergalactic prices of food and drink from any on-site stall. At least Dick Turpin was honest about his highway robbery.

Accessories

Festival ticket	Well, duh.
Water bottle (reusable)	A simple one will do. You're not an England rugby player, so you don't need one of those high-sided squirty ones.
Tent	
Mallet or hammer to bang in tent pegs	In the spirit of terrible puns, all mallets must be known as 'Timmy' and all hammers as 'MC'.
Sleeping bag	
Folding chairs	You'll look like a pensioner on the beach at Margate, but who cares?
Day pack/knapsack	
Flip-flops or sliders	Your feet will need air, but you will not necessarily want to go barefoot.
Toilet roll	
Sun-tan lotion	Yes, it'll probably rain. Yes, it's better to have lotion and not need it than to need it, not have it, and end up looking like a tomato-engorged lobster. Oh, and make sure the SPF is at least 30.
Hat	For the same reason.
Waterproof jacket	For the opposite reason.
Contraceptives	As with sun-tan lotion, better to have it and not need it rather than vice versa.
Sunglasses	Hope springs eternal. Depending on their design, you can look either like an 80s porn star or an international cricketer.
Headtorch	You'll look like a miner. It'll be worth it. Headtorches are unbelievably useful.
Earplugs	Not just to deaden the incessant music but to allow you to sleep through the 5am arguments from the next-door tent. Alternatively, use noise-cancelling headphones. In extremis use noise-cancelling headphones over earplugs.
Plastic bags	You can never have too many plastic bags. Food rubbish, dirty clothes, various other unmentionables. They're environmentally unfriendly, sure, but after four days at a festival they're not half as environmentally unfriendly as you are.
Gaffer tape	Unbelievably useful for mending snapped tent poles, tears in tent fabric, holes in wellies etc. In extremis, can be used on the gobshite in the next-door tent who won't pipe down even though it's 5am.

Portable phone charger (preferably solar)	You could just do without your phone for a few days, but in this day and age that's like asking someone to do without a limb. But in the spirit of not bringing anything you're not prepared to lose…
	… consider leaving your smartphone at home and bringing an old model. As long as you can text or call, that's really all you need. So you can't video the performances? Good. Watch them with your own two eyes instead rather than via a screen which will give rubbish playback quality anyway.
Food	Cereal bars, dried fruit, crisps: things which won't go off and which will give you a quick energy boost when you need it (which will be almost always).
Drink	You'll be thirsty. Rest assured you won't be the only person undergoing the 'Can A Man Survive For 96 Hours On Red Bull Alone?' challenge.
Paracetamol/ ibuprofen/aspirin	Do we really need to spell out why?
Wet wipes	Like plastic bags, you can never have too many.
Toothbrush and toothpaste	At least ensure that your mouth smells nice when your armpits have long stopped being your charmpits.
Hoodie	Evenings can get cold. Yes, we sound like your mum. Deal with it.
Cash	Trendy London shops might only take electronic payment, but at festivals cash is still king.
Swiss Army knife/ Leatherman	You're bound to need at least one of the blades at some stage, and as a bonus you can pretend you're Ray Mears or Bear Grylls.
Wellies	You will need wellies, whoever you are. Cheap ones which cost a tenner, brand name ones at 10 or 15 times that price, brightly patterned ones or traditional green/navy blue/black, thigh-high waders, turquoise ones nicked off the Cambridge Boat Race crew: any of these are better than none of these.
Camping stove	Hot meals during wet weather, or cups of tea at any time, can make the difference between misery and ecstasy.
Cool boxes	The reverse applies. Warm beer on a hot day is dispiriting. Cold beer on a hot day is manna from heaven.

The golden rule of festival attendance, and if you only remember one thing from this book then make it this – don't take anything you're not prepared to lose or damage (including, or perhaps especially, your friends).

Choosing your route

However you choose to travel to the festival, be aware that it will almost certainly take you a lot longer than you think, and that the extra time will be right at the end just before you reach the festival location. When the Singularity comes and the machines take over, even all the quantum computing power in the world still won't be able to find a way of getting people into (and out of) a festival arena without miles of tailbacks and hours of waiting.

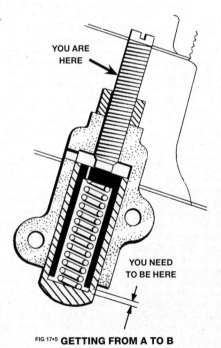

YOU ARE HERE

YOU NEED TO BE HERE

FIG 17•5 **GETTING FROM A TO B**

i) Car
In some ways the easiest, as it allows you to bring more stuff (planes have baggage weight limits and trains limited luggage space.) Sharing a ride with friends (or even strangers found on carshare apps/social media websites) can split the cost and make the journey pass more quickly (or more slowly if you fall out over what music to play, which in itself won't bode well for several days at an, er, music festival.)

ii) Coach
Some festivals organise coach services from big cities to their location. Be prepared for some wally to be listening to 'National Express' by The Divine Comedy so loudly on their headphones that you can hear it clear as day (albeit rather tinny).

iii) Train
Book early – really early, like months in advance – to get the best deal. Leaving it too late, especially on main intercity routes, can mean you having to fork out the equivalent of a small country's GDP for a ticket. Check the festival website for information about shuttle buses to and from the nearest station.

iv) Hitch-hiking
Have a word with yourself. This isn't the 70s any more.

⚠ What not to take

Air horns They're the most annoying things in the world, and if you persist in using them then sooner or later you will find a fellow festival-goer keen to discuss the rectal mechanics of air horn insertion with you. And guess what? You'll deserve it.

Animals Support dogs apart, of course.

Fireworks They're bad enough on Guy Fawkes Night and at New Year. In all other circumstances, they're unforgivable.

Flares The bright fiery things which whizz up into the air, obviously, not bell-bottomed trousers. The latter are always welcome at festivals, not least as a reminder of their 60s, and 70s, roots.

Generators If those around you wanted to be near something noisy and belching out diesel, they'd have stayed in Europe's largest car park (or, as it's better known, the M25).

Anything made of glass It will break. You will stand on a shard in bare feet. You will cut your foot open. The wound will get infected by one or more of the approximately 82,847 pathogens in the mix of mud and sewage. You will at best need the leg amputated. It's not worth it.

Megaphones See air horns.

Guitars You think you're Bob Dylan. You're not. The last thing people want after days and days of music performed by professionals is your drunken, off-key and out-of-tune strumming.

Laser pens Dangerous and really stupid.

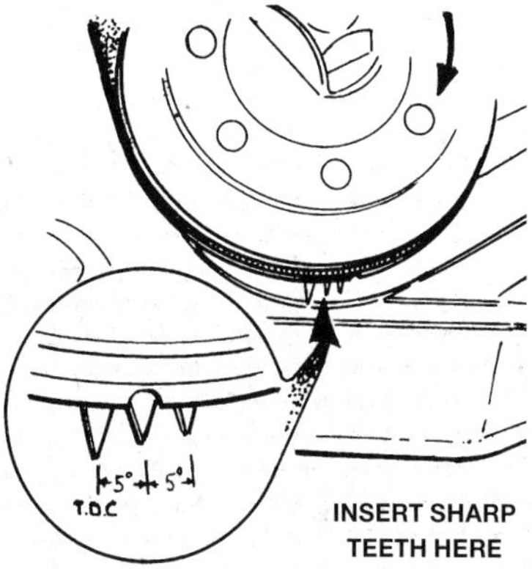

INSERT SHARP TEETH HERE

FIG 17·6 **GOOD FOR OPENING TINS. BAD AROUND INFLATABLE MATTRESSES**

Anything the festival website says you shouldn't bring. Some of the prohibitions may seem petty or unreasonable. Ask yourself whether they'd still seem so if everybody brought the banned items in question.

Pimping your ride

Festival fashion for the lady

Fringed suede waistcoat
The look: carefree wood sprite (or perhaps geriatric cowgirl depending on age and rate of wear and tear).

Daisy Duke hotpants
There's a reason they're called Daisy Dukes, and that's because she wore them so well. Beware any item of clothing named after its most iconic wearer, as it'll almost certainly look better on them than it does on you.

Glitter
A good idea at the time. Less so when you're still finding it in and on obscure parts of your body two weeks after the festival ends. Since traditional glitter is made primarily from microplastics, and is therefore due to be banned from many UK festival sites starting in 2021, more environmentally friendly alternatives will become increasingly popular.

Sequined bodysuits
There will be photographic evidence of this, so sure, if you don't mind that – and you're not intending on ever running for public office – then go for it.

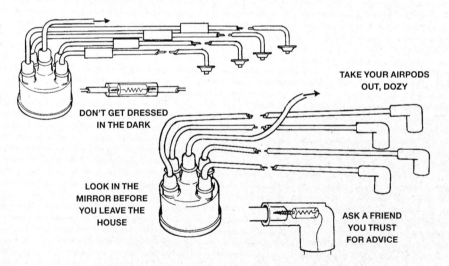

TAKE YOUR AIRPODS
OUT, DOZY

DON'T GET DRESSED
IN THE DARK

LOOK IN THE
MIRROR BEFORE
YOU LEAVE THE
HOUSE

ASK A FRIEND
YOU TRUST
FOR ADVICE

FIG 17•7 **MAKING SURE YOU'RE PROPERLY ACCESSORISED**

⚠ Fashion Dos and Don'ts

✔ **DO** take a bum bag. Yes, they look faintly ridiculous, and are more usually the preserve of American or Japanese tourists, but they're incredibly useful.

✘ **DON'T** wear heels. They'll get stuck in the mud/grass/coir matting/gap between stage panels, and when they get stuck so too will you.

✔ **DO** wear a bucket hat. They're practical, on trend, and exhibit a decent amount of ironic self-awareness.

✘ **DON'T** go shirtless. Few men look as good as they think they do without a top on, and the ones who do by definition appear insufferably smug and way too in love with themselves to give anyone else a look-in.

✔ **DO** dress for varying weather conditions. Crowded House may well have had a festival in mind when they sang 'Four Seasons In One Day'.

✘ **DON'T** wear a mankini. They were funny once, briefly, when Borat was in his heyday. That window has long since been slammed shut.

✔ **DO** try some face paint. YOLO. (That's 'You Only Live Once' in youth-speak, Grandpa.) Also, do remember to remove it before the sweat and dirt do it slowly, messily and in the manner of a psychotic clown for you.

✘ **DON'T** dress in any kind of costume you might also run the London Marathon in. The same issues – heat, itchiness, cumbersomeness etc. – will afflict you as it would the hardy marathoners, and you won't even have the 'doing-this-for-charity' glow.

✔ **DO** give a wide berth to anyone wearing a onesie, a Viking outfit, tweed, or cross-dressing.

✘ **DON'T** wear a band's shirt to their gig. This is deeply uncool. The only thing more uncool is to have bought the shirt just now at the merchandise desk so it still has the fold creases in it (and doesn't have kebab/beer/unidentified bodily fluids on it).

✔ **DO** get rid of your festival wristband when you leave the festival. Within the confines of the festival, it's obviously mandatory. Outside, it looks sad, try-hard, and a desperate attempt to get someone to ask you what it was like.

Tie-dye

Making one of its perennial comebacks. If you look hard enough, you should have an item or two at the back of the wardrobe from the last time it was fashionable. Vintage clothing in general is always a reliable festival look, not just for its haze-of-nostalgia nod to the countercultural movement of yesteryear but also because it's more environmentally friendly to keep using old clothes than to buy new ones.

Bohemian robes

Good for making you look like an extra from a Wicker Man remake. Bad for not scooping up three metric tonnes of mud on the hems.

Slip dress

Easy, versatile, cool in a hot dance crowd.

Fisherman's vest

You know, those multipocketed ones which have always been the refuge of the serious nerd, geek, or fisherman. Now apparently co-opted as cool by the on-trend festival goer. (In certain South American countries they are apparently favoured dress items of the local gang cartels, but the crossover between Latitude attendees and Guatemalan coke bigwigs is, we hope, minimal.)

And for the male driver

No. Just don't. Jeans, trainers, T-shirt, the holy trinity of old favourites. You can't go too far wrong there. No, mate, you won't look amazing, but you won't look like a total bellend either.

OK, if you insist. A nice patterned shirt and decent cut-off jeans shorts. But that's it, you hear? And if you want to know what you'll look like by day three of a festival, there's an easy way to find out. Run ten miles while making sure to eat a doner kebab at every odd-numbered mile and drink a pint at every even-numbered one. How you look at the end of that run is a harbinger of your festival future.

SUPERGLUING A PATCH ONTO YOUR JEANS....

.... AS YOU NEVER LEARNT TO SEW

FIG 17•8 **EMERGENCY FASHION DIY**

Looking after your valuables

a) Take cash and keep it safe. Some vendors will take cards, others won't.

b) Keep valuables in a money belt around your waist, or at the very least in secure pockets (i.e. not shallow baggy ones). Front pockets are better than rear ones. Don't leave valuables in your tent.

c) Sealable sandwich bags. Ideal for putting phone/money/credit cards/other valuables inside. Keeps them dry not just from rain but also sweat, sticky drinks, beer and other, ahem, fluids.

d) To preserve mobile phone battery life, turn all the phone settings down to minimum (contrast, volume, brightness), turn vibrate off, and stay off social media/e-mail/the internet. The whole point of going to a festival is to escape all that stuff anyway, isn't it? The real world will still be there when you get back, don't worry.

e) At night, take a headtorch. There are small models which easily fit in a pocket and yet are easily bright enough when you need them.

f) Counter-intuitively, don't padlock your tent when you leave it. That will just signal that you have stuff worth nicking, and it's a moment's work for a thief with a sharp knife to slash through the fabric and get in that way.

g) Make sure your tickets are genuine – that is, buy them either from the festival itself or a reputable trader. If you get an e-mail saying 'Glasstonberry tikets here good price honest guv', think twice. (Actually, don't think twice. Just delete.)

WARNING

Don't make any major life decisions at a festival. Your mind will be in an altered state, be it naturally or chemically. You will be tempted to jack in your job and tell your boss all the things you've been dying to tell him for years. Like many things, this will seem like A Good Idea At The Time. Sleep on it. If it still seems like a good idea in a fortnight's time* then maybe it might be worth considering. (*It won't.)

17

Camper vans

When choosing a festival tent, remember that sizes are for adults only and do not include the vast amount of gubbins and paraphernalia required to sustain you for the duration of the festival. Go at least 50% up: i.e. two people in a three-man tent, four people in a six-man tent etc. Otherwise you'll have to leave rucksacks etc. outside your tent, where they'll get (a) wet (b) nicked (c) both.

When it comes to tents, two skins are better than one (and no jokes about four skins, so you can just keep those thoughts to yourself). A pop-up single-skinned tent may survive a gentle drizzle, but serious rain will cause it (and, by extension, you inside it) huge problems.

If you're in a group with multiple tents, stake out your ground like cowboys of old used to when they circled the wagons. Strategically placed chairs and blankets around the outside will set up a buffer zone not much less heavily fortified and contested than the DMZ between North and South Korea.

Remember the old adage: 'My friends suggested we go camping. Things I need. 1. New friends.'

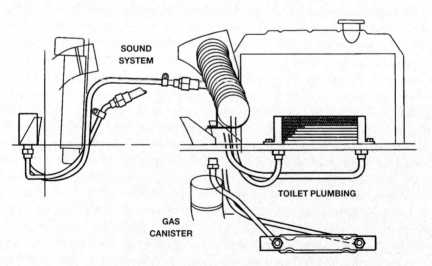

FIG 17•9 **THE IMPORTANCE OF THE RIGHT CONNECTIONS**

⚠ How to pitch your tent

1) If need be, go to outdoors shop and purchase tent. Set aside several hours to indulge fantasies of being Chris Bonington and lovingly stroke all the gear in the shop incl. crampons, ice axes, thermonuclear bivouacs.

2) Set aside several more hours to argue with wife about the catastrophic waste of money said purchase represents, and several further weeks to argue if you dare suggest that the tent will come in useful 'for, you know, when we go camping together in future.'

3) Arrive on site. Remove tent from car. Ignore smirks from nearby campers who see that the tent bag is spotlessly clean and that the tent has therefore clearly not been used before.

4) Unpack bits of tent from bag and lay neatly on ground.

5) Turn bag upside down in attempt to find instruction manual.

6) Realise instruction manual hidden somewhere within tent fabric.

7) Spend ten sweaty and increasingly exasperating minutes trying to find manual.

8) Having found manual, realise that the diagrams bear no relation whatsoever to anything you have on the ground.

9) Attempt to fit tent poles together. Snap a couple in frustration. Be glad you've brought gaffer tape. Realise that bringing gaffer tape might be the sole triumph of this entire process.

10) Wrestle with getting main body of tent up. Find that it's like changing a duvet cover to the power of 100. Wonder if anyone's ever died while trapped in a semi-erected tent. Accept that you may be making history.

11) Realise you've forgotten something with which to bash the tent pegs into the ground. A beer can will do. Waste of good beer, naturally, but needs must.

12) Finally get tent up, to sustained if insincere applause. Realise you've lost your body weight in sweat.

13) Silently abandon plans to be next Chris Bonington.

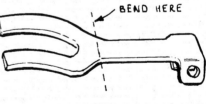

BEND HERE

I BROUGHT THE
BOTTLE OPENER

FIG 17•10 **BAD NEWS: IT DOESN'T
DOUBLE AS A TENT PEG TOOL**

Parking

Where to pitch your tent

Somewhere high. If a field is sloping, make sure you're at the top of the slope. That way, when it rains your tent will collect less water than those further down the hill. Also near a landmark if possible (preferably one which isn't going to move during the festival...).

Where not to pitch your tent

Anywhere near a stage, a main footpath, food stalls or – especially – toilet blocks. Any of those equal people and smells. People equal noise, and drunkenness, and general annoyance. Thomas Hardy may have had festivals in mind when he wrote Far From The Madding Crowd. As for smells, well, you can use your imagination.

Remember where your tent is

Put something distinctive and visible on it as a marker, such as a flag. Not a cross of St George or a pirate flag, as everyone has those. A novelty helium balloon on a long string might be a better bet. (Remember to anchor it, obviously, or be prepared to see it floating merrily off into the great blue yonder and leaving your tent as anonymous and hard to find as it was before.) Trying to locate the damn thing in a sea of identikit fabric is hard enough in any circumstances, let alone in the small hours when it's dark and you've had a skinful. Climbing into somebody else's tent is unlikely to go down well at the best of times, and, as we have already established, this is unlikely to be the best of times.

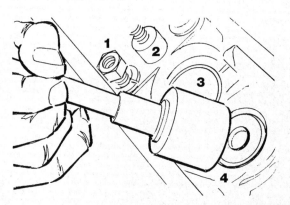

1. *IT'S AROUND HERE SOMEWHERE*

2. *MAYBE THIS ROW INSTEAD*

3. *SORRY, DIDN'T MEAN TO WAKE YOU. BIT PISSED*

4. *THE HELL WITH IT. THIS ISN'T OURS BUT IT'LL DO*

FIG 17•11 **GEOSPATIAL TENT LOCATION AFTER HEAVY DRINKING**

⚠ A sea of flags

No music festival is complete without a sea of flags. For the festival-goer, a flag can be many things at once. It can be a marker to help you find your tent, or your friends, or both. It can be a vehicle of self-expression. Or it can confirm to everyone within a five-mile radius that you are a complete bellend.

It goes without saying that the more distinctive your flag is, the better. If you are going to write a slogan on it, for the love of God make it funny or sweet. The Glastonbury one with a picture of festival founder Michael Eavis and the caption 'Summertime Santa,' for example. Or a flag saying 'Ban Flags', or 'Flaggy McFlag Face', or 'False Flag' (nice combination of existential conundrum and political commentary), or the hardy perennial favourite 'Orgy Here'.

The length of the flagpole is almost as important as the flag itself. In general, the longer it is the better. This makes your flag more visible and, when held up in the crowd at one of the stages, won't obscure the view of those behind you. (Hold up a long flag attached vertically to the pole, on the other hand, and be prepared to learn some new Anglo-Saxon words while being told to get in the sea.)

A longer pole also means the flag is harder to keep steady, which in turn will work your arm and shoulder muscles, which in turn will in some small way offset the shattering lack of exercise and the monstrous abuse through which you're putting your body for the duration of this festival. The Festival Workout, if you will. It's not quite Jane Fonda or Mr Motivator, granted, but even they had to start somewhere.

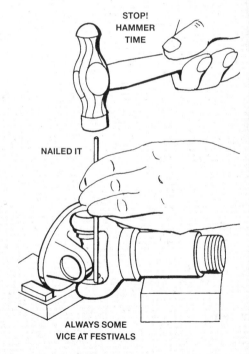

STOP! HAMMER TIME

NAILED IT

ALWAYS SOME VICE AT FESTIVALS

FIG 17·12 **PUTTING YOUR FLAG UP**

Exhaust systems

Few two-word phrases can strike as much fear in even the sturdiest heart as 'festival toilets' (though 'surprise exam', 'just married' and 'Ann Widdecombe' are also up there). Festival toilets are not so much an ecosystem of their own as a new dimension beyond the normal rules of space and time. In the movie *Event Horizon*, when the crew of the eponymous spaceship go through a black hole and stumble across hell, it's entirely possible that they've ended up inside a toilet block on the final day of a festival in high summer. Quite why UN inspectors went to the Middle East to search for biological weapons is anyone's guess: every summer entire weapons of mass destruction are created not far from the A303.

The human digestive system being what it is, however, you will almost certainly need to use the facilities at some stage during proceedings – and, to quote the peerless Australian mockumentary Kenny, you may well encounter 'another classic example of someone having a two inch arsehole and us having installed only one inch piping.' There is no way to make this a pleasant experience, but there are at least some ways to ensure that it's not a total disaster. And remember that for the vast majority of the world, the stench and primitive nature of such toilets are entirely commonplace and not merely confined to a few days every year.

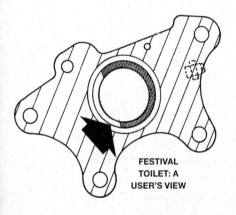

FESTIVAL
TOILET: A
USER'S VIEW

FIG 17•13 **THE GATEWAY TO HELL**

WARNING

Beware – be very ware – of anyone loitering round the back of the Portaloos with intent. It's not unknown for young men in particular to enjoy playing 'Push Over The Porta' with one of their friends inside. This will, of course, only be a problem for you if you are that friend, or if you're mistaken for that friend. You will stink either way.

Know what you're dealing with

a) Chemical toilets

Know what kind of toilet you're dealing with. Chemical ones will at least have some sort of flush mechanism to transport the waste away, though they are equally easy to block up – there's always someone who uses half a toilet roll per visit.

b) Long drops

Long drops or slurry pits are just what they say they are: a raised platform with a hole and a seat above a pit dug into the ground. The metal cubicles for the latter often have no roof, which at least mitigates some of the worst of the smell. If in a long drop, the three words to remember above all others are as follows: Don't. Look. Down. And if by chance you drop something into the slurry pit – lighter, lipgloss, mobile

FIG 17•14 **LEVEL 42: WHEN YOUR CHEMICAL TOILET NEEDS EMPTYING**

phone, watch, pint of beer – for the love of God don't attempt to rescue it. To paraphrase every Eastenders character whenever a fight's about to kick off: 'Leave it! It ain't worf it!'

Many slurry pits are emptied every day, or at least every other day, so if you time your visit right it may be slightly less pungent than usual. And console yourself with the fact that at least you don't have to do that job.

c) Compost toilets

With festivals increasingly keen to demonstrate their eco credentials, compost toilets are becoming ever more popular. Each cubicle has a compost bin beneath it, and you're supposed to add a scoop of compost to every deposit you make. The unholy trinity of human poo, toilet paper and compost will eventually make 'humanure'. Listen, I don't think of these names.

⚠ Top toilet tips

1) Toilets closest to main stages and/or thoroughfares will have the longest queues and the most egregious levels of filth. Find ones away from the beaten track.

....

2) Bring your own toilet paper. Most festivals do provide some, but often it'll be the cheapest and nastiest brand imaginable, with a texture almost exactly equidistant between aluminium foil and sandpaper.

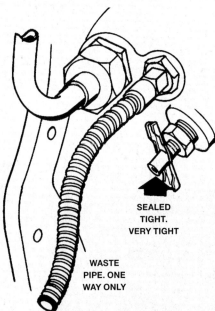

SEALED
TIGHT.
VERY TIGHT

WASTE
PIPE. ONE
WAY ONLY

FIG 17•15 **FESTIVAL TOILETS: THE GIFTS THAT KEEP ON GIVING**

3) Try to avoid touching anything once inside the toilet. Easier said than done, granted, but elbows can be pressed into service to lock doors and press flush buttons, and if you have moderately strong thigh muscles you can simply hover above the seat and all the foul demons beneath it.

....

4) Don't wear a jumpsuit, playsuit or onesie in a festival toilet. You'll need to take it off in order to, ahem, ablute, and that's more or less impossible on three separate grounds: there's not enough space, part or all of it will inevitably end up dangling in something unmentionable, and by the time you've managed to get it off you'll have asphyxiated on the fumes. Playsuits and jumpsuits seem like the perfect outfits to take to a festival.

....

5) Go during daylight hours if you can. Pitch Black In A Portable Toilet is a horror film waiting to happen.

....

6) Breathe through your mouth. If need be, squirt or smear something strongly scented under your nose: perfume, Olbas oil, Vicks vapour rub, whatever.

7) Some toilets have no seat, comprising two footplates and a hole in the ground. Those who've been travelling in India and certain parts of France will be used to them. Assuming your thigh muscles are up to the task of holding the squat, this is actually the most hygienic option due to minimal contact with surfaces which have themselves come into contact with other people's skin.

....

8) Hand sanitiser. You can never have enough, not at a festival.

....

9) If you really can't stick the toilets but are still determined to go to the festival, then consider using Imodium and/or eating the worst kind of junk good imaginable, devoid of fibre or anything else which usually helps you start a new movement.

Proper working, flushing, non-chemical toilets. Not unless you're the most VI of VIPs. You have to be at least a VVVVIP, and very possibly a VVVVVIP, to merit a toilet vaguely akin to the one you have at home. Unless you're royalty or Kanye, forget it.

Additional info for men

For men, there are always urinals too. Increasingly these can be found not just side by side but also in clusters around a central pillar, thus technically allowing people to converse while urinating. The word 'technically' is important here. No gentleman should ever strike up a conversation with another gentleman not yet of his acquaintance while one or both of them are standing tackle out. Nor, of course, should they attempt to shake hands.

EYES STRAIGHT AHEAD. ONE HAND ON THE OLD FELLA, THE OTHER IN YOUR POCKET

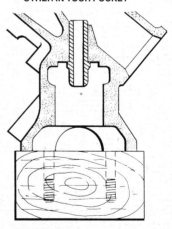

FIG 17•16 **URINAL ETIQUETTE: A SHORT GUIDE**

Driving your vehicle

Planning

Check out the festival programme in advance and make a note of which bands you really want to see. (Remember your mum going through the bumper Christmas edition of the *Radio Times* circling all the films she wanted to watch? That.) Then you can see if any of them clash with each other (it's a shame that The Clash have disbanded, otherwise you could say: 'Oh no, we can't go and see Coldplay, they clash with The Clash) and plan accordingly. In the army they say that no plan survives first contact with the enemy, and Mike Tyson famously said that 'everyone has a plan till they get punched in the mouth', so it's entirely possible that your own plan will be derailed by alcohol, narcotics, incompetence or all three, but at least the thought was there. (Also, don't plan too much. It's not a school trip where everything has to be scheduled to the minute, and timetables are for buses. Leave lots of time free for going wherever the fancy takes you. You'll almost certainly stumble across an act you've never heard of which you'll love.)

Medical

Know where the medical tent is. People get sunstroke at festivals, and trench foot too (if you manage to get both at

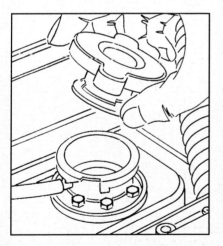
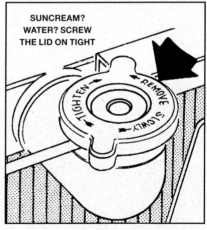

SUNCREAM? WATER? SCREW THE LID ON TIGHT

TIGHTEN

REMOVE SLOWLY

FIG 17•17 **FLUIDS AND CONTAINERS**

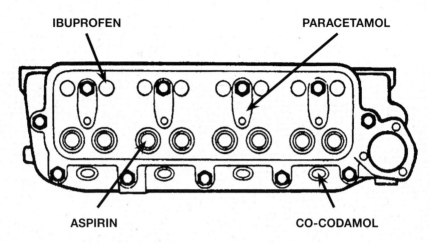

IBUPROFEN   PARACETAMOL

ASPIRIN   CO-CODAMOL

FIG 17•18 **FIRST AID KIT: THE ESSENTIALS**

the same festival, good effort). Dehydration, whether or not linked to a hangover, can also be a problem, as can any MPIs (Mystery Pissed Injuries) which are there when you wake up but which you have absolutely no recollection of getting. A basic first-aid kit is your friend here: plasters, bandages, sun cream, prescription medicine, and lots of ibuprofen.

Acceptance

You will smell. You won't sleep well. You'll spend a lot of your time in queues. Moaning or complaining about any of these won't make them any better. Either accept that this is how it's all going to turn out or don't go in the first place. Besides, everyone there's in the same boat (literally,

probably, given the state of English summertime rainfall). Embrace it and imagine how blissful the first bath back in civilisation will be. You can lie in warm soapy water and ponder the most pressing question in your life: put your festival clothes through five consecutive washes, or simply incinerate them?

Pale colours

We know this is total sacrilege if you're a Goth, but dressing all in black on hot sunny days is a shortcut to heatstroke. White or pale colours are best. Yes, you will look like Lionel Richie c. 1984 and/or Miami Vice. Sorry. Also: natural fabrics in loose-fitting garments rather than man-made fabrics in tight ones.

Vehicle types

The One... With The Giant Flag	Yes, giant flags are good. But not when they're held by a bloke who's drunk so much he can hardly stand up, and who keeps knocking into other people with the pole and then apologising
The One... On Someone Else's Shoulders	Yes, she (it's almost always a she, unless an Olympic weightlifter's in the crowd and can therefore support a full-sized adult man on his shoulders) is having a great time. She's waving her hands in the air like she just don't care. The TV cameras love her. But you're right behind her and you can't see a damn thing. Get down and watch from ground level like the rest of us, woman.
The One... Who Brings The Kids	The kids don't want to be here. Every adult not related to them doesn't want them to be here, not just because this is an adult festival (not in that way, or at least not until 2am when everyone's had a few) but because there's a place where kids can go without washing for days on end and be lumped together with a whole load of people they've never met before, and that's boarding school. Leave your kids at home (with proper supervision, obviously) or go to a proper family-friendly festival with them.
The One... Who Tries To Crowd Surf	It's never the sylph-like gymnastic ones, is it? It's always the overweight and drunk ones, and if you're unlucky enough to be in their path you'll find that it's like trying to manhandle whale blubber.
The One... With All The Gear And No Idea	New tent. New wellies. Pristine cooking equipment. A fold-out trestle table with enough plates and cutlery to feed the five thousand. Don't worry. After four days of monsoon conditions have made this not-so-quiet corner of England resemble the Somme, they'll be down to everyone else's level.
The One... Who's Always Filming	They're always filming the band. They're always filming their friends. They're always filming their friends watching the band. For the love of God, put the phone down, just enjoy the moment and trust in your memory.
The One... Who's Always On Social Media	A close relative of The One Who's Always Filming. Live streaming to Facebook (which is the reason no-one else can get any data, as they've nicked the entire festival bandwidth). Filtered and curated shots to Instagram. (No-one should be allowed to use the word 'curate' outside a museum.) Silly rabbit ears and love hearts to Snapchat. Thanks Apple/Samsung/other phone manufacturers for unleashing this particular form of hell on us.
The One... Who's Got His Shirt Off	And the only six-pack in evidence is the one he's just guzzled. When he comes into contact with you, which he inevitably will, it will be like trying to push away a buttered pig.

The One... ***Who's Always*** ***Trying To Blag***	There's nothing they won't try to get for free and nowhere they won't try to get into. Food, drink, accessories, backstage passes, and every time holding everyone else up with their ten minutes of bantz/negotiation/haggling. Mate, it's not going to happen and you're not funny. Give it up.
The One... ***Who Knows*** ***All The Lyrics***	Not just the choruses, which everyone does, but all the lyrics. Of the most obscure songs. Of the most obscure band. And sings them, very loudly and very out of tune. Right in your ear. There are few instances in which homicide is entirely justifiable, but surely no right-minded jury would convict you for this.
The One... ***With All The*** ***Wristbands***	Previous festivals, this festival, random charities, and so on. You can hardly see their arm, they have so many wristbands. They will almost certainly suffer some sort of freak accident: a pulled ligament when one or more of these 4,392 wristbands catch on a fence, or gangrene in the arm due to reduced blood flow, or some sort of vile rubber allergy.
The One... ***Who Takes Too*** ***Long Doing*** ***Selfies In The*** ***Giant Frame***	There's a queue for this, as there is for everything. Everyone thinks their poses are both original and hilarious, which may be true, but to paraphrase George Bernard Shaw 'the hilarious bits are not original and the original bits are not good.' And just when they're about to leave they see a friend 100 yards away and call them over and repeat the whole process again from the start. Get in the sea, all of you.
The One... ***Who's A Hippie***	Of indeterminate age, as they're now so pickled by drugs that the usual strictures of time and bodily wear and tear have long since ceased to apply. They were definitely at the original Isle of Wight festivals half a century ago, though of course they can't remember much about it.
The One... ***Having A*** ***Meltdown***	They've lost their friends. They've lost their money. They've lost their tent. And now, several drinks to the wind, they're crying big snotty tears about it. In essence, they've reverted to being a teenager. It will pass.
The One... ***Who Hunts*** ***As A Pack***	University-age men, usually, all dressed in ironically loud shirts and knee-length shorts. They're loud and drunk and laugh like a pack of demented hyenas. Individually, they're all perfectly pleasant and intelligent. En masse, they're boorish morons.
The One... ***Who Makes It All*** ***About Them***	Shouting loudly, waving a sex doll, dressed in a morph suit or a mankini. Everyone they've ever been to school with, or university with, or worked with, remembers them. Everyone also rolls their eyes and makes an internationally recognised hand gesture signifying that the subject is no stranger to self-pleasure.
The One... ***Who Forgot*** ***The Suncream***	This guy is so red and pulsing that you can see him from the other side of the festival. Hell, you can probably see him from space. If he fell asleep in the sun, his mates will have written 'DORK' in sunblock on his back.

Model history

6th century BC

The Pythian Games in Delphi are held in honour of Apollo, the god of music (not to be confused with the Apollo space programme, Rocky's rival Apollo Creed, or electronic dance band Apollo 440). In the spirit for which festivals will many centuries hence become famous, drinking contests go hand–hand with the music.

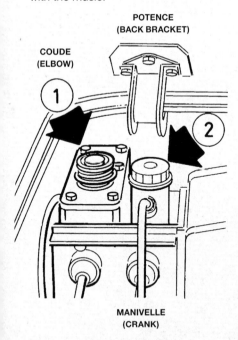

POTENCE (BACK BRACKET)

COUDE (ELBOW)

MANIVELLE (CRANK)

FIG 17•19 **OLD SCHOOL FESTIVAL EQUIPMENT**

1914

Classical composer Rutland Boughton establishes a series of concerts, lectures and recitals called the Glastonbury Festivals. Well, you've got to start somewhere. Someone asks Rutland where the nearest mosh pit is. He does not understand the question.

1961

Harold Pendleton, founder of London's Marquee Club, sets up the National Jazz and Blues Festival in Reading, later to become the Reading Festival. This makes it the oldest continuously held popular music festival in the country: a little ironically, perhaps, given that Reading itself is sometimes seen as lacking excitement.

1968

Following the previous year's Monterey festival in the US (and a year ahead of Woodstock), and tapping into the hippie culture of free love, environmentalism, anti-establishment, creative freedom and so on, the first Isle of Wight festival takes place. A small island accessible only by boat, rather conservative and most famous for a week in which men in gold-buttoned blazers traipse on and off yachts and call each other 'commodore': what could be a more natural place for a festival than this?

1970

Michael Eavis hosts the first Pilton Pop, Blues & Folk Festival, later to become Glastonbury. Tickets are £1, but you got free milk from the dairy at Worthy Farm. Why yes, that does make you feel old. And slightly bereft of hope for the future, too.

1971

Glastonbury features the first incarnation of the Pyramid Stage. It's built from scaffolding and metal sheeting, and sited over a blind spring found through dowsing. Textbook Somerset. Performers include David Bowie, Traffic, Hawkwind and The Worthy Farm Windfuckers, who inexplicably never make it as big as the other three.

1981

Glastonbury makes a profit for the first time. Eavis donates £20,000 to the Campaign For Nuclear Disarmament (CND), the start of a long tradition of charity donations.

1985

The rain falls on Glastonbury, and falls, and falls. Since Worthy Farm's a dairy farm, what washes down into the low-lying areas is not just water, and not just mud, but liquid cow dung too: knee deep in front of the Pyramid Stage. Or, as festival-goers like to think of it, quite a clean year, all things considered.

1994

Channel 4 televise Glastonbury for the first time. An unknown band called Oasis play on a minor stage: a collector's item in that the Gallagher brothers are still talking to each other.

2000s

The internet and streaming services cause a huge shake-up in the music industry. With recorded music now available for next to nothing, bands have to find different ways of making money – and fans want to hear their favourite bands live. The festival scene continues to grow and grow.

2012

Glastonbury takes a fallow year to coincide with the London Olympics, because there aren't enough Portaloos in Europe to service both. This is not a joke.

The 1980s were a great decade for music, but not for festivals: indie, punk and new wave didn't really sit well with the festival ethos, and MTV encouraged pure pop music. The nearest thing to festivals were probably raves, unofficial dance gatherings in fields.

Model types

There are hundreds of festivals, and these are just ten of the biggest and/or best-known ones that you can go to (or perhaps that you can do, as increasingly people seem to be talking about festival-doers rather than festival-goers: 'Are you doing Glastonbury this year?'

1) Glastonbury

The daddy of them all. Not the oldest, but the biggest and certainly the most iconic, to the extent that 'Glastonbury' is almost a shorthand for music festivals in the same way 'Hoover' is for vacuum cleaners and 'Durex' is for condoms.

(The latter is more prevalent than the former at Glastonbury and indeed most other music festivals, that's for sure.) It's televised on the BBC and raises money for Oxfam, Greenpeace and WaterAid.

2) Isle of Wight

Relaunched in 2002 after effectively being banned in the early 1970s. Much less counterculture than it was originally.

3) Reading

Percentage of attendees who've just finished their GCSEs: 30. Percentage of attendees who've just finished A-levels: 30. Percentage of attendees who've just finished their degrees: 30. Percentage of attendees who normally feel quite young and all, working in normal office environments with a wide variety of ages, but who now feel as though they have one foot in the grave: 10.

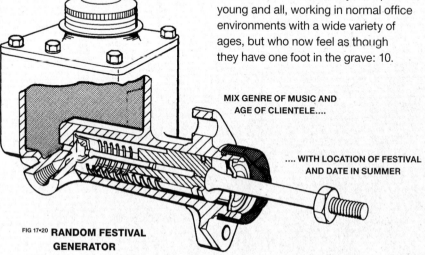

MIX GENRE OF MUSIC AND AGE OF CLIENTELE....

.... WITH LOCATION OF FESTIVAL AND DATE IN SUMMER

FIG 17•20 **RANDOM FESTIVAL GENERATOR**

4) Bestival

The last big festival of the season, taking place in September on the Isle of Wight (but nothing to do with the Isle of Wight festival itself). It's fun and wacky and in general a happy place, which is after all what most festivals aim for!

5) Camp Bestival

The children-friendly version of Bestival, which takes place in Dorset rather than on the Isle of Wight. You take the little ones there and use that as collateral for the time a few years from now you want to spend a week at some Croatian trancefest and parcel them out to friends, no ifs no buts, of course Mummy loves you darling, but now she has to go and take a load of Es and pretend that she's the age she was when you weren't even the tiniest of twinkles in her eye.

6) Latitude

Very Suffolk, in every way. If Richard Curtis (himself a Suffolk resident) designed a festival, it would be a lot like this: 'a bit like a giggly, middle-class barbecue that has got slightly out of control' according to author Michael Odell. There are author talks, drama classes and Royal Shakespeare Company performances to go with the music, and the campsites are separated from the main arena by a lake and forest.

7) Download

Held at Castle Donington, and the second biggest festival in the country after Glasto. Metal, punk, classic rock – it's got something for everyone as long as you like it Spinal-Tap-going-up-to-11 loud. Often said to be the friendliest festival of all, without ego, pretension, snobbery or rivalry. No-one tries to look cool at Download: they're just there for the music and the company.

8) T in the Park

Scotland's most famous festival. Began in 1994 and named after its main sponsor, Tennent's brewery. (Only in Scotland...)

9) Creamfields

A predominantly dance festival as opposed to rock/pop/indie/folk etc. – which is unsurprising given that it grew out of the Cream DJ nights in Liverpool. If you want big-name DJs, this is the place to come.

10) V

Sponsored by Virgin, and often the first festival that many people go to, so it's commercial and 'safe'. The acts are often well-known and the facilities are very good. One critic described it as a 'festival for people that don't actually like music but still want to say they have been to a festival', which is rather harsh and says as much about the snobbery of some festival-goers as it does about V.

Further guidance

a) Before you set out, take some empty large milk cartons, fill them three-quarters full with water and freeze them. Then put them in cool boxes alongside your food. They'll keep your food cooler for longer and also provide you with drinking water as the ice melts.

b) If outside alcohol is banned and you want to smuggle some in – not that we're suggesting you do, you understand, but drinks at festivals often necessitate taking out a second mortgage – then vodka in water bottles is always a good way (remember which is which, obviously), as are wine bottles inside hollowed-out baguettes. Several festivals now ban ticket holders from bringing alcohol onto the premises.

c) Tall friends are worth their weight in gold. They can see further than you can to spot where queues might be shorter, and you can see them from a long way away so you know where to find them.

d) Get there early. The traffic will be lighter, there'll be fewer people, and you'll have a better pick of spots in which to pitch your tent.

e) Pack ruthlessly. When you have everything you need laid out neatly on the bed (you do that, right? Don't just bung it into the rucksack willy-nilly?), halve it. Seriously. Festivals are no frills. Fringes on your on-point cowgirl waistcoat, perhaps, but no frills.

f) Leave no trace. When you leave the festival for good, take everything with you. Yes, there are professional clean-up personnel who'll be spending days picking up rubbish: why add to their task?

g) Arrange an emergency meeting point when you arrive. People's phones run out of battery and/or the local network gets overloaded so messages don't get through. Go back in time and do what people did before mobiles – i.e. used some initiative. Food stands and large signs or flags which won't be moved are good options. Unless you've lost your sense of smell, the toilet blocks aren't.

h) To get to the front of the crowd, come in from the side rather than the middle or back. Call out a random name repeatedly to make it look as though you're trying to reach a friend who's already there.

Conclusion

On a Friday night in August 2018, staff at a nursing home in Schleswig-Holstein discovered that two of their elderly male residents were missing. The police were called and search parties were mobilised. It was not until 3am that the men were found...

...at Wacken Open Air, the largest heavy metal festival in the world. Headline acts included Judas Priest, Hatebreed, In Flames, Running Wild, Arch Enemy and In Extremo. So much beer (400,000 litres) is consumed at the festival that this year the organisers installed a four-mile beer pipeline to cope with the demand.

A beer pipeline! Wars are fought over natural gas and oil pipelines: maybe one day the good citizens of Schleswig-Holstein will take up arms to defend their right to have premium-quality lager sent through pressurised tubes at a constant temperature and flow rate for the delectation of their hop-attuned taste buds.

Anyway, we digress. According to the newspaper *Deutsche Welle*, 'the men, who were disorientated and dazed, were reluctant to leave the festival, so police escorted them home with the help of a taxi and a patrol car.'

Well played, ageing metalheads. Well played indeed. This is very much how we should all aspire to get old.

Then again, they were in good company at the festival. Rob Halford, lead singer of Judas Priest, was 66 at the time: the Misfits, who were also playing, have among their ex-members the 63-year-old Glenn Danzig, and the members of Germany's own Destruction are all in their 50s. (Destruction is one of Germany's 'Big Four' thrash bands, along with Sodom, Kreator and Tankard).

Most countries or sectors have a Big Four one way or another. Britain has HSBC, Lloyd's, Barclays and the Royal Bank of Scotland. Accounting has Deloitte & Touche, PriceWaterhouseCoopers, Ernst & Young and KPMG. Japanese motorbikes have Honda, Kawasaki, Yamaha and Suzuki. Technology has Amazon, Apple, Facebook and Google. But only Germany has Destruction, Sodom, Kreator and Tankard.

The lesson of the wacky Wacken wanderers is surely the simplest and most obvious one: you're never too old for a festival.

Titles in the Haynes Explains series

Now that Haynes has explained Festivals, you can progress to our full-size manuals on car maintenance (which include a few camper vans), *Outdoor Survival Manual* (take it with you), *Sleep Manual* (something you'll need after the event), *Sheep Manual* (follow the crowds) and *Build Your Own Electric Guitar Manual* (instead of the air version).

There are Haynes manuals on just about everything
– but let us know if we've missed one.

Haynes.com